The Seeds All Turned to Dust

The Seeds All Turned to Dust

Copyright © 2022 Jake Graham
All rights reserved.

ISBN 978-0-6456224-2-3

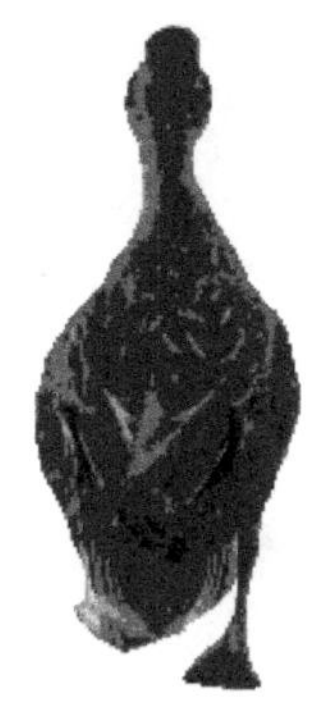

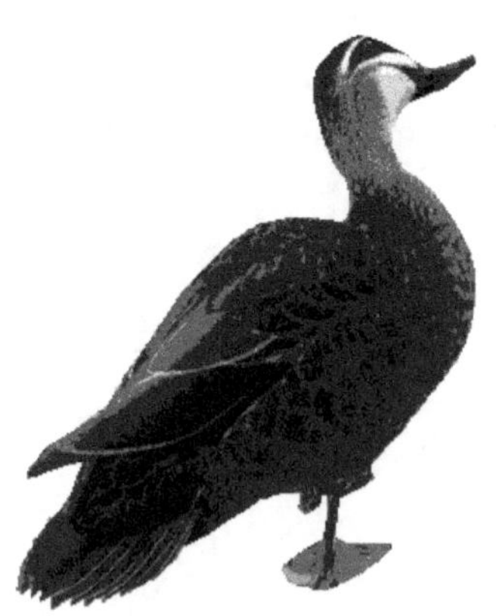

The Seeds All Turned to Dust

Blue Rose

The blue roses grow in a field by the river
Their petals and stems tall and proud
A cool breeze blows, makes the butterflies shiver
Their wings flick with colours so loud

The sun shines so bright in a cloudless blue sky
Reaching out with its warmth and light
The birds above sing happy songs while they fly
And say "everything will be all right"

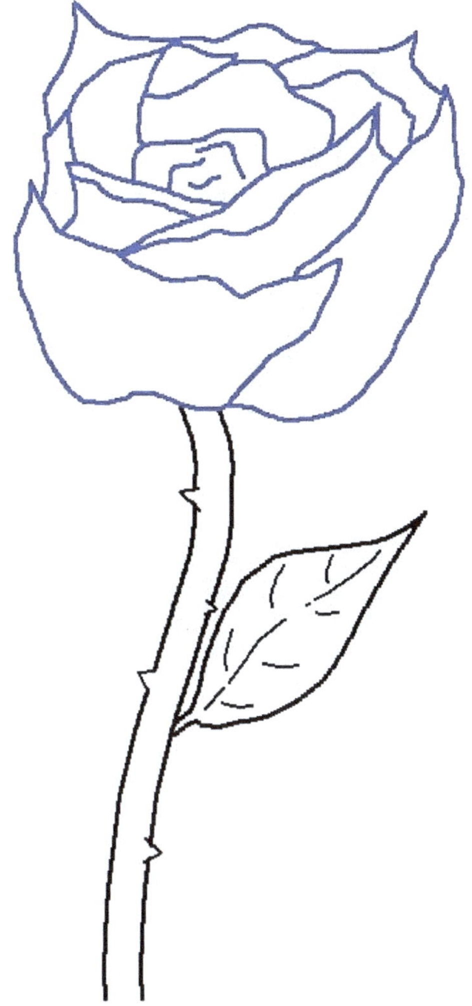

Overload

Distortion of the senses
No filter to keep me bound
I would never try to hurt you
But I seem to anyway
And those words don't ever fade

Erasure of the memories
No lists to keep them straight
I try to hold on to them
But they still dissipate
And I'm left here to wait

Confusion of the feelings
No formulas to check
I try to make sense of them
But then I just get lost
And it isn't worth the cost

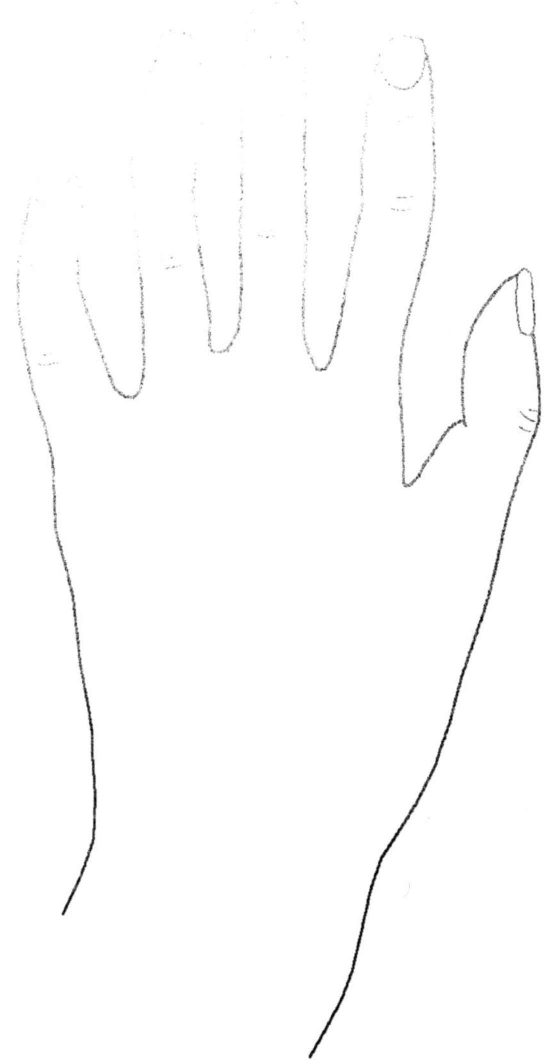

When Winter Comes

When winter comes
we have such fun
huddled with books by a fire
Resting on rugs
Hot chocolate in mugs
What else could you ever desire?

When snow falls
I hear the call
of a peaceful, coveting quiet
like the misty days
that float away
the dreams we have in private

Frost covers grass
it shines like glass
with a thousand shimmering jewels
like the clouds that fly
ever passing by
and a chilling breeze, so cool

Look at the snow
a pearly-white glow
covering earth like a blanket
like icing on cakes
small glittering flakes
this wonderland feels so enchanted

Snowmen stand proud
all part of the crowd
Winter's army coming to play
like frozen friends
may the fun never end
on this beautiful wintery day

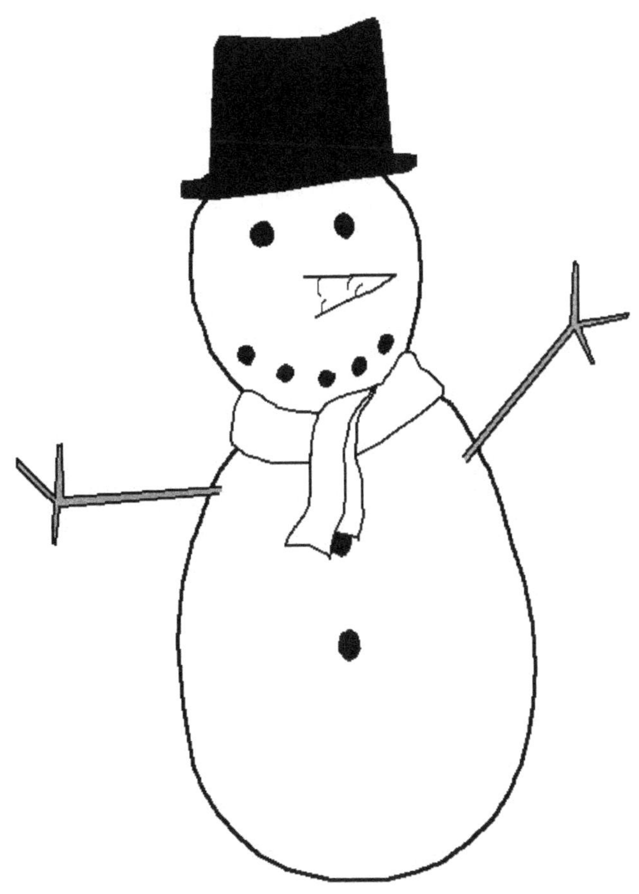

Held

I can't think about an embrace
without remembering your arms
and every feeling that flowed through me
realising you meant no harm
And I think about just how much
it scared me to feel safe
after years of fear and flinching
at the thought of an embrace

I can't think about your comfort
without remembering your pain
and the mess I had created
while escaping from my brain
And I thought about just how much
safer I felt with you
than any place I'd been in years
Your comfort gave some truth

I can't think about your kindness
without remembering your heart
and every beat I felt project itself
in the early morning dark
And I wondered just how much
you knew about that time
or the days and weeks that followed
with your kindness on my mind

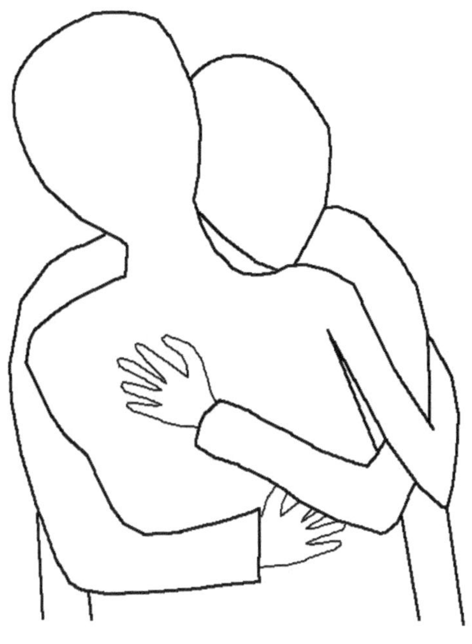

Petrol Station

I'm running on fumes of a feeling from days ago
and I won't find a place to reload
because feelings aren't as easily found
as a petrol station somewhere down the road

Nearing closer to empty on a feeling I held
from a moment coming closer to lost
I'll wrap myself up in a blanket, so tight
and forget if it's worth what it cost

A warning light flashes to signal the end
From vivid to hardly there at all
I slipped from your grasp in an instant
but I hope you'll catch me if I fall

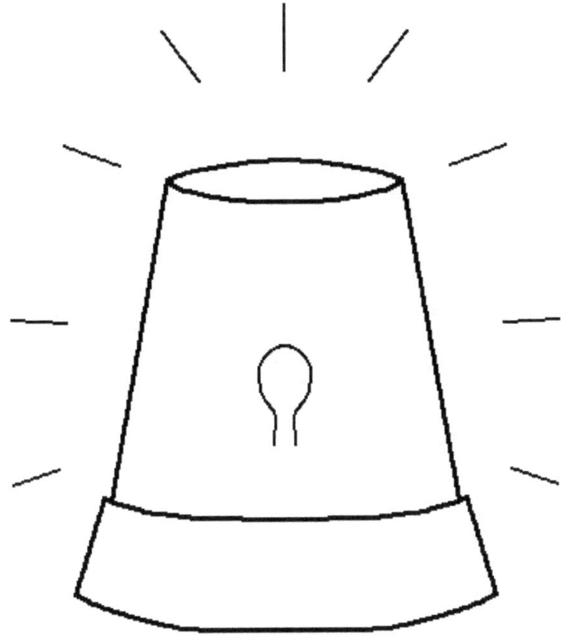

Bruised

I went from feeling nothing
To feeling everything at once
And it feels like I'm imploding
As concrete fills my lungs

I can't blame you for it
Though you might be the cause
Hold me close at night
While I reflect on all my flaws

I want to understand you
Wonder how I could begin
Don't think that I could start to
Show these thoughts I hold within

I don't know how to speak aloud
Thoughts that obstruct my mind
Not sure what to feel about
Comfort you helped me find

But even in your safety
I'm clouded and confused
And worry that you'll hate me
When parts of me are bruised

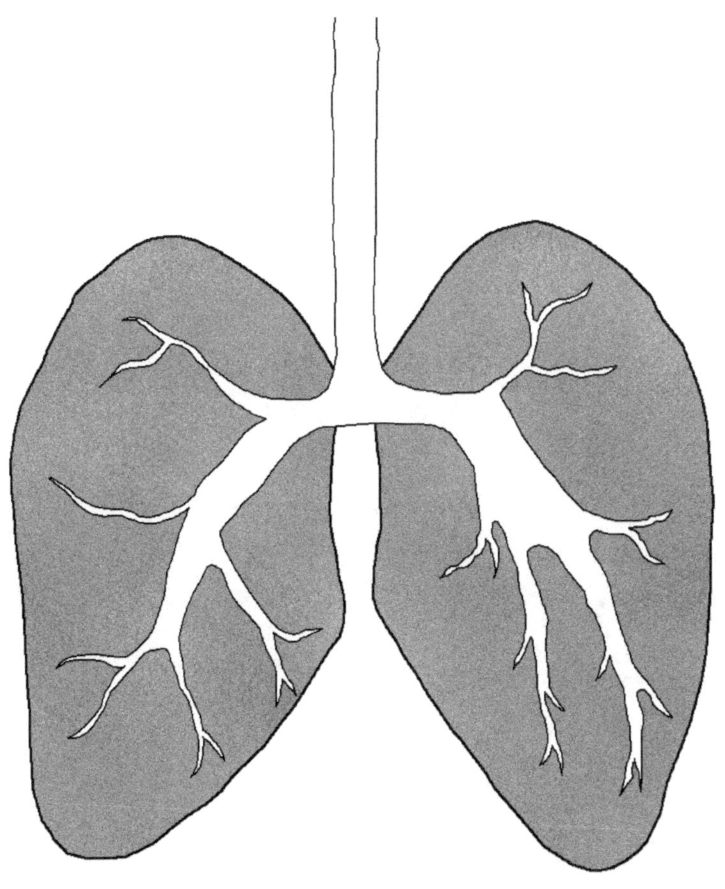

Can't You Tell?

Can't you tell I'm giving up
on everything you've said to me?
Every lie, every promise
All those twisted fantasies

Can you see I've had enough
of the heartache that you cause?
So many nights of broken glass
of shouting, slamming doors

Can't you hear exhaustion
in my voice with every word?
Every sentence, crying out
pleading to be heard

Can you feel the pain I hold
in these shaking hands?
So many days of hateful words
breaking up our plans

Can't you taste the bitterness
that's dripping off your tongue?
Every word, every statement
you've shared since I was young

Can you listen to me
as I'm pleading with you now?
So many years of cruel, harsh taunts
but you never broke me down

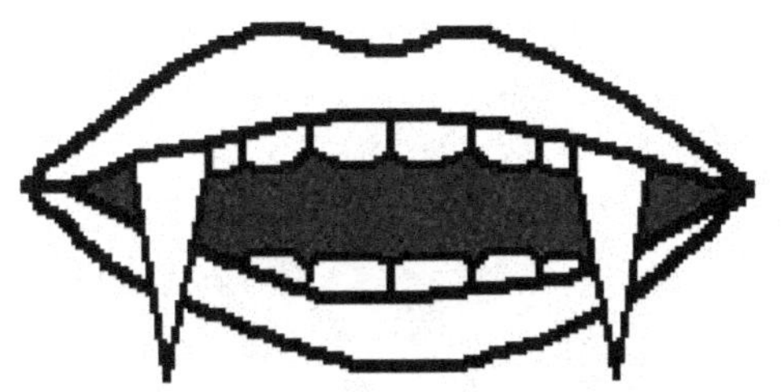

Only

Only in the pit of night
would silence fall
and make things right
Only in the depths of day
would you hear the words
that could make you stay

Only in the trials of sorrow
would you await
a new tomorrow
Only in your happiness
could something break
to mend a mess

Only in the hollow dark
would madness cry
out like a lark
Only in the clearest light
could something wrong
make things alright

Trails of Thought

Sometimes I don't know
how to explain what I'm asking
because somehow, somewhere between
the office in my brain where things are written
and the mailbox for communication
my thoughts,
like a post van joyride,
get lost
and only on occasion
can they be found again
for in those moments the diversion
was simply a detour

But others are simply gone
and they won't be found again

So if it is my fate
to pose queries of nonsense
forged by an overlap of multiple trails of thought
then it is a fate I shall be willing to accept

For it is me

And,
if nothing else,
it certainly does keep things interesting

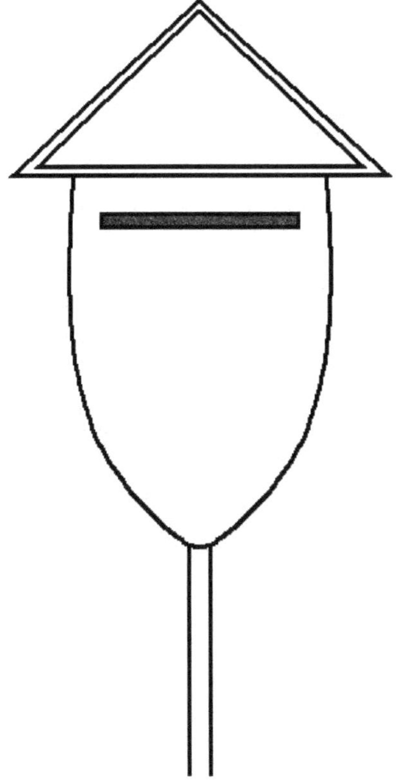

The Evening Poet

All of my thoughts are now coming in rhymes
At moments, exhausting to think in these times
Now I'm going out to collect in my washing
Just taking a break though, I am not stopping
Perhaps why I don't often read poetry
Is I find myself rhyming and longing to be
Ah, bugger these spiders! My shirt's not your home
Maybe you could reside in the trees that have grown
I've collected it all, now I'll head back inside
Though what is for dinner I still must decide
If I were to skip it, I think to myself,
that would do such terrible things to my health
So I'll heat some baked beans, potato gems too
then I'll sit down and watch something all the way through
But I'll watch it without you, because you are sick
I hope you recover and feel better quick
Now dinner is done, the movie is finished
My chances of staying awake are diminished
So I'll head to bed, dream of us together
and know that I'll be right here for you forever

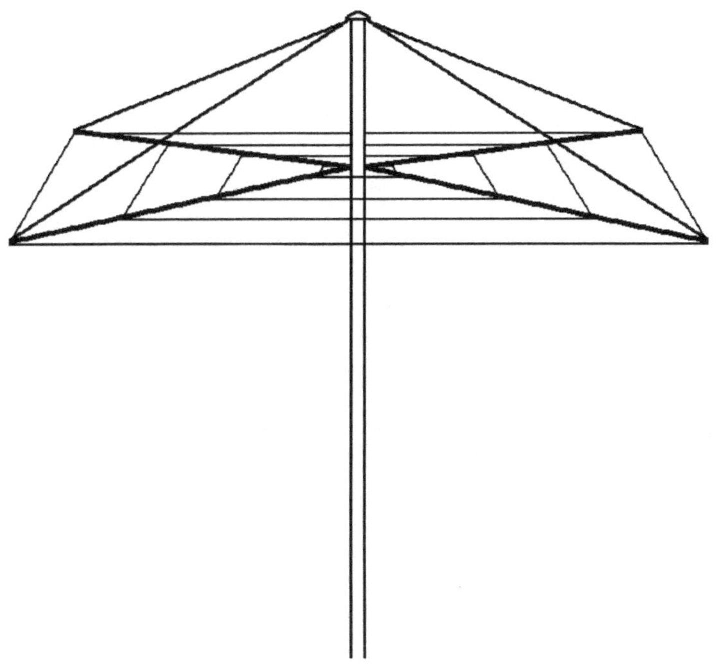

Today I Feel

Today my body sounds like an old haunted house
Its inner structures creak and they groan
Vibrations through skin like footsteps of a mouse
Encumbered by feeling alone

Today I can hear only whispers of dreams
Their feelings run cold in my chest
Electricity in fingers like wires on beams
Ecstatically feeling suppressed

Today I can taste all the blood from my past
It floods me like an old hotel hall
Reminding myself that these moments don't last
Gripping ropes that burn as I fall

Today I can smell the fear drenching my soul
It covers me, inch upon inch
Converting to energy, reaching for a goal
Transporting with a truck or a pinch

Today I can feel every hand that I've touched
and those that touched me in return
The singular moments don't seem like too much
but combined they ferociously burn

Today I can see all the visions of people
that made contortion seem so straight
A balancing act verging on illegal
but everyone else thought was great

Today I feel naught but contempt left for you
and all you've managed to achieve
For despite evidence to accompany truth
and your known ability to deceive
and witnesses, and history too
Your lies, they still choose to believe

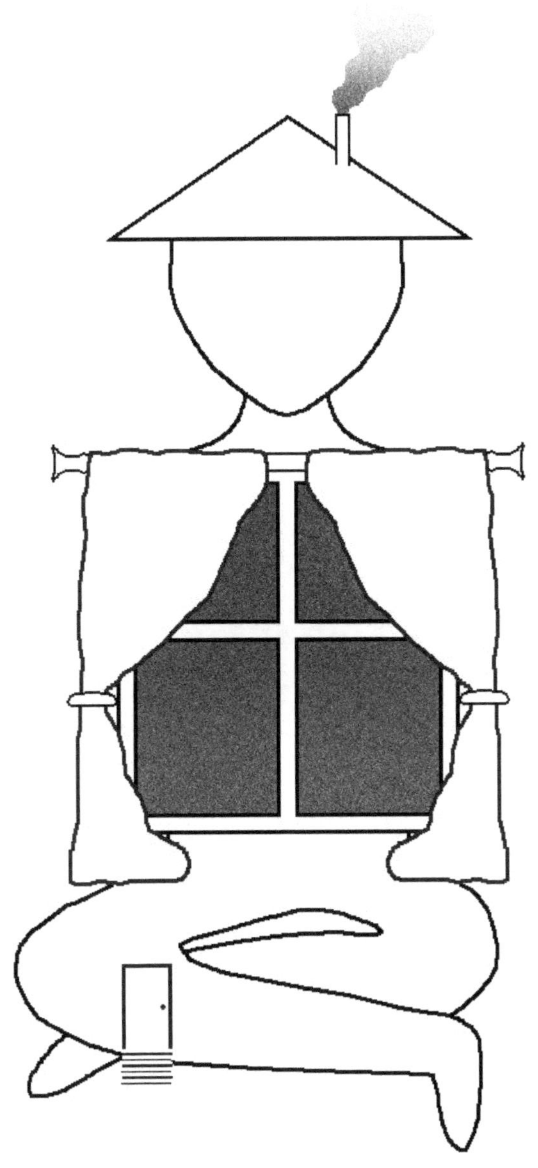

I Hear

I hear your words spoken,
so viciously vain
as I trudge through the sunshine
and days without rain

I hear your lies uttered
so horribly cruel
as I move like an old car
that runs low on fuel

I hear your threats echoed
so violently loud
as I picture your drunk grin,
always so proud

I hear your facts twisted
so blatantly wrong
as you convince all the rest
it's my fault I'm gone

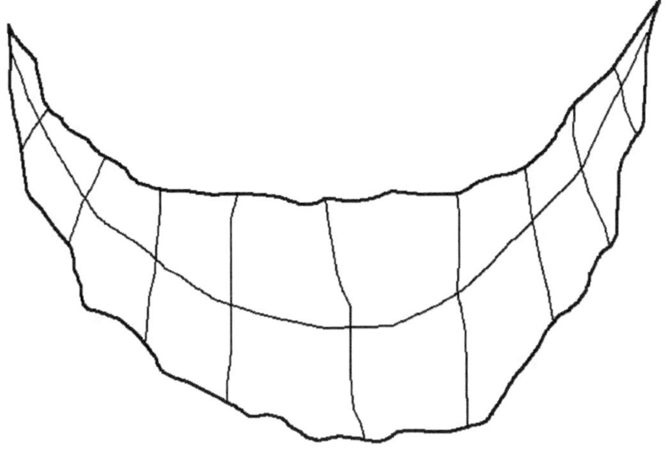

Snail Soliloquy

Oh to be a snail
and hide inside my shell
But then I would not see
the footsteps coming toward me
to crush me in their path
because I was there
because it was raining
and snails like the rain

Oh snails!
With those little wiggly bits
that sprout from their heads
and then retract
to grow and shrink
and retreat back into the head
as a snail does with its shell
and as I do with myself

SNAILS!
Wiggly! Slimy! Fantastic!
To be home wherever you are
Travelling anywhere, near or far,
not needing to ever return
The snail went on a journey,
a trip to see great things
The snail, moving, saw many
There was so much to learn
and once it was over
they'd no need to go back
Searching endlessly
for an end
and the end of the journey
was that

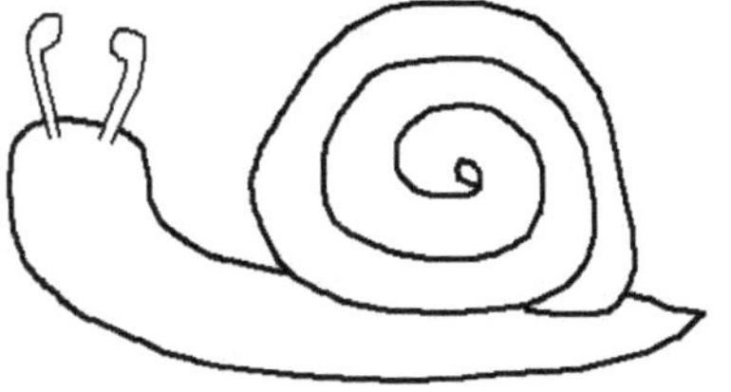

Fight

Every breath is an abrasion on reality
Every dream is a falling star
We can fight for what we want to be
but never who we are
And thoughts we have that disappear
are struggling to return
Our needs can be our greatest fear
Our wants we can unlearn

Every step is a scratch on my soul
Every beat is a cracking glass
We can run forever to catch our goals
but never change the past
And hopes we have that rearrange
are sometimes hard to find
Our lessons can be found with change
Our peace with passing time

Every word is a scar in the depth of me
Every memory a crushing blow
We can alter who we hope to be
but never what we know
And if my past has served me well
(though I know it has not)
I'll be the tale I live to tell
because I am all I've got

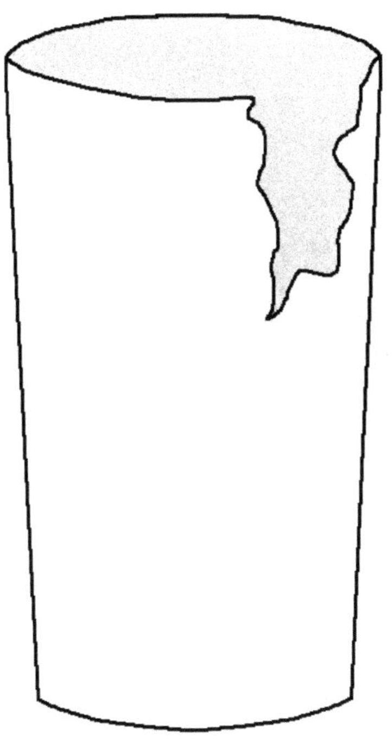

Dissociation

We're on the freeway doing 40
The other side runs normal at 110
a visible form showing
what it feels like to dissociate
Where it feels like parts of me are running
at less than half speed
while everyone around me
runs as they always do
Like my brain got caught in slow motion
while everything around runs on 2x
and the harder I try to catch up
the further I fall behind

All I can do
is
watch
as the world keeps moving around me
as life goes on without me
and I'm sitting here
waiting
as if attending a film at the cinema
But this isn't a film,
this is LIFE.
MY life.
And I am merely an observer.
An outsider.
A witness to my own movements and breaths

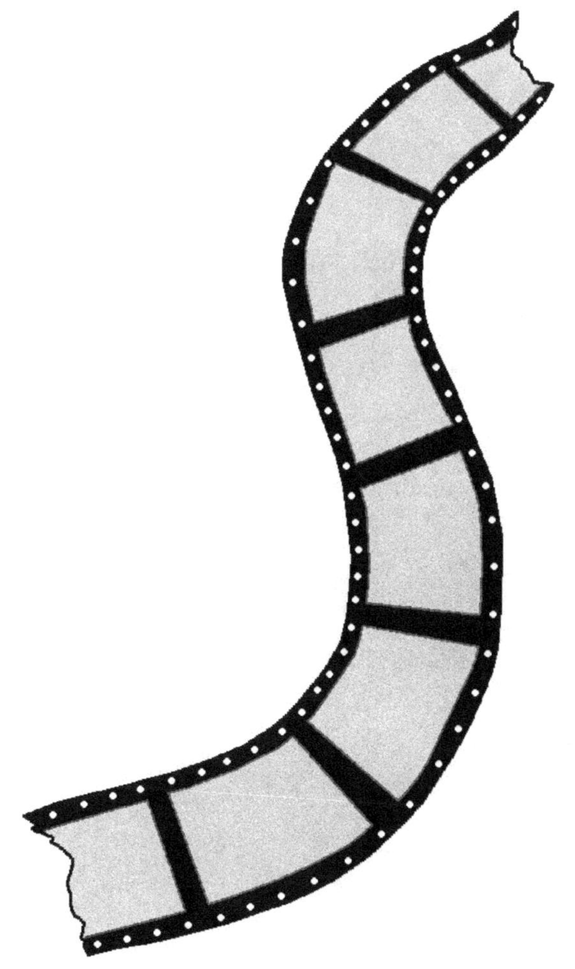

Violence

Is this what you wanted?
A circumstantial death
A dress upon my body and
a rope around my neck
Salty liquid drips
in rushes down my chin
while screams of empty hatred
tell me all I am is sin

Is this what you wanted?
A moment of relief
A pause in wasted anger and
a break to clenching teeth
Gravity is pulling
me back toward the floor
while you look at all I'm doing
and still say there should be more

Is this what you wanted?
A life consumed by lies
A cessation of innocence and
a break in the disguise
Crimson droplets flood
like flickers of my soul
while every new piece drained just takes me
closer to my goal

Is this what you wanted?
An end to all that's said
A weight of guilt upon you and
a memory of the dead
Purgatory's calling
my name as I fade out
while you watched everything happen
and claimed to side with doubt

Was this what you wanted?
A feeling lost in time
A missing piece within me and
a man excused of crime
No room for forgiveness
for all that has been done
While words became as violent as
a bullet from a gun

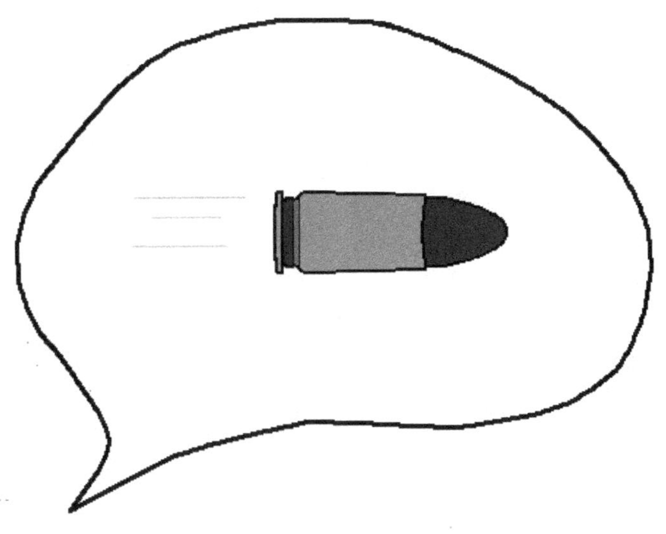

Sound

A dull hum isn't background noise
but background noise is a dull hum
Footsteps, sniffing, somewhere a door is opening
Conversation, rattling keys, and whistling of electricity
A vacuum, a thump, general background static
Heating running through the vents, impending silent panic
The breaths of those around me, as well as my own
A drawer moves abruptly and its inner contents moan
And faces,
so many faces,
are moving all around
as if their ears are not encumbered
by a plethora of sound

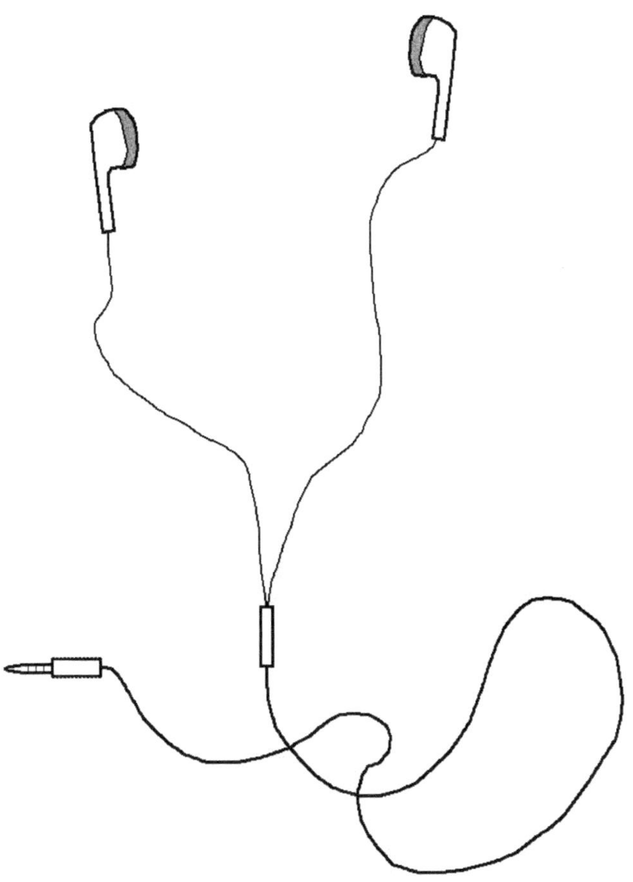

Despite You

You fooled me with your kindness
to deceive me with your lies
Your words were cruel and heartless
Your drinks your alibis

You tricked them with excuses
Dismissive of the pain
and everlasting bruises
you plastered on my brain

You challenged me with falsehoods
to others, and to myself
Your actions showed where you stood
Your threats showed how you felt

You convince them with laughter
Gift them with fake hope
That means nothing to me after
your goal to see me choke

You broke me down with cruelty
and violence in your words
Vindictiveness eludes me
despite the hate you've stirred

Through all your petty teasing
Through all your lies and threats
Through all your people-pleasing
You'll one day pay your debts

Through all your manipulation
Through all your slamming doors
Through all your justification
You'll lose what you fought for

Through all your deceiving
Through all your bans on rights
Through all your twisted grieving
You'll one day lose your fight

Through everything I suffered
Through every harsh word thrown
Through every aging moment
I am the one that's grown

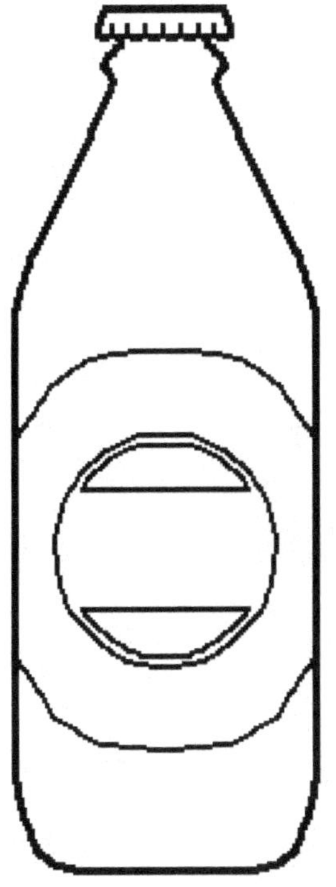

Loss

I said I couldn't stand
to watch you fall apart
So you forced me to sit
and ran into the dark

I said I couldn't stomach
the thought of losing you
So you made me close my mouth
when you said we were through

I said I couldn't bear
another broken soul
So you handed me a roll of tape
and shattered all I know

I said I couldn't handle
losing you once more
So you locked me out for good
when you pushed me out the door

I said I couldn't trust
the things you said to me
So suddenly you turned around
and ran with your deceit

I said I couldn't cope
with the games you'd play
So you made a final choice
and you threw me away

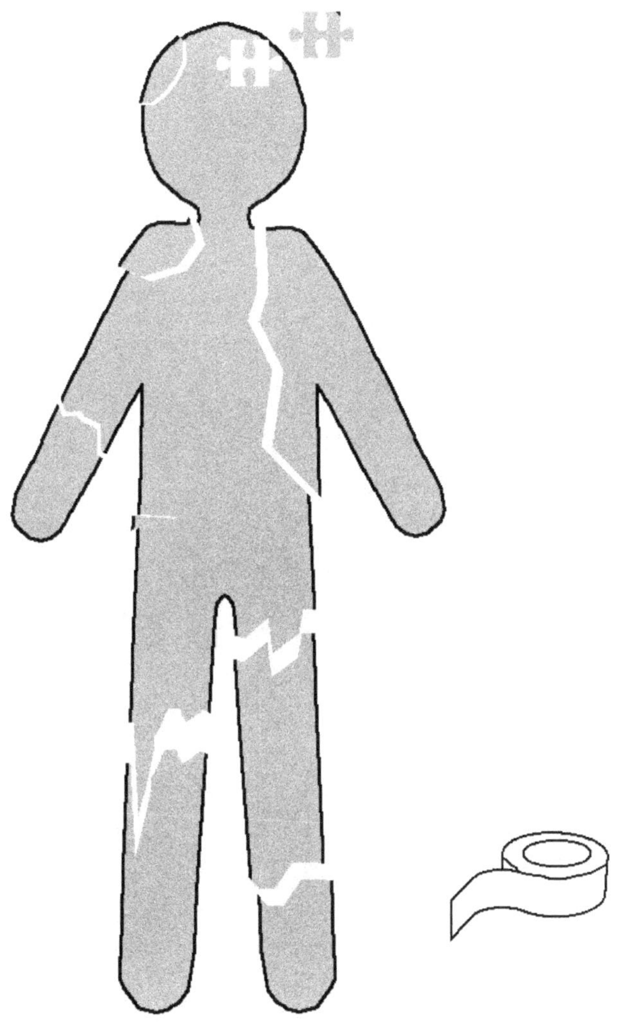

Happy Words

"Go write something happy"
What if I don't know how?
What if the crease is permanent
in my ever-furrowed brow?
I don't believe in happy
Not what you want to hear
I'm good at disappointment
and living through my fear

"Write something that's less dark"
What if it can't be done?
What if the darkness lives in me
and swallows all my fun?
I understand the dark things
and they understand me
I'd rather write things how they feel
than pressure just to please

"I can't stomach your writing"
Then my words are not for you
I write because I feel the words
The things they form are true
Not everyone understands
or feels everything the same
I think that's half the point of art
We don't do it to be tame

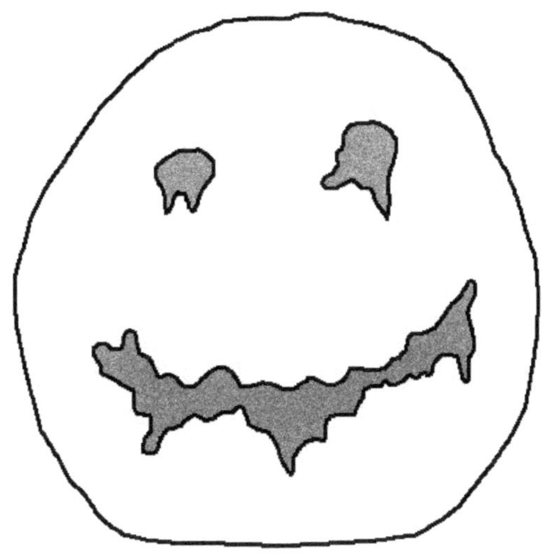

Snail Soliloquy: A Second Sliming

Oh to be a snail
So genderqueer and void
For then I would not feel
the dysphoria that haunts me
and burrows in my bones
because they can shift
because sex is fluid
and snails just don't care

Oh snails!
With their exoskeletons
that rest on their backs
to hide inside
and travel with
A skeleton that is a home
and helps keep you together
as mine sometimes feels to me

SNAILS!
Gooey! Trailing! Wonderful!
To not care for gender at all
No pressure to conform, large or small,
just being your slippery self
The snails climbed up a window,
to escape from the rain
The snails, high now, could stay dry
Tomorrow they'd go down
and head to the garden
back where they tend to live
Without gendered rules
confining them
inside a skeleton house
or shell

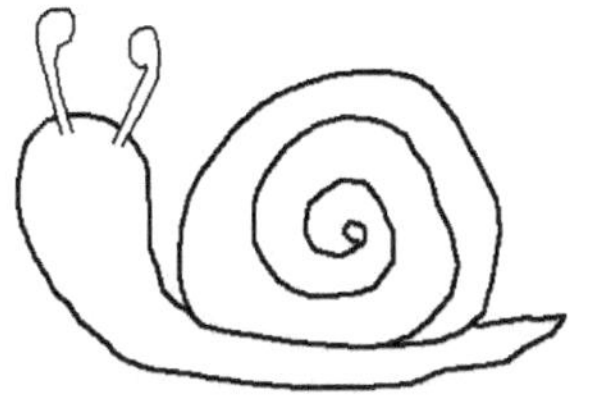

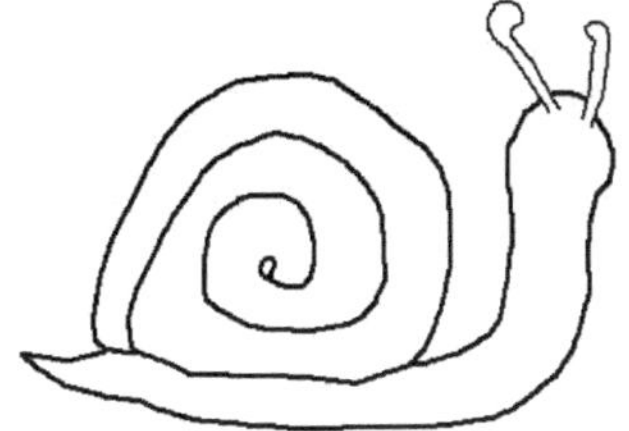

Friend

We don't talk a lot these days
I'm not sure we ever did
and sometimes we go away
and look for places that we hid
But we always find ourselves
just as we were before
Save me from my own hell
and I'd ask for nothing more

We don't talk a lot at times
and it works for us, it seems
While I'm busy forming rhymes,
you keep busy building dreams
But we never take steps back
to take breaks from stepping forward
Encourage me to stay on track
and I don't feel ignored

We don't talk a lot at all
but we never needed to
Like a net under a fall
help me to not slip through
But there'll always be struggles
Something to make us fight
Though it's never too much trouble
to find another light

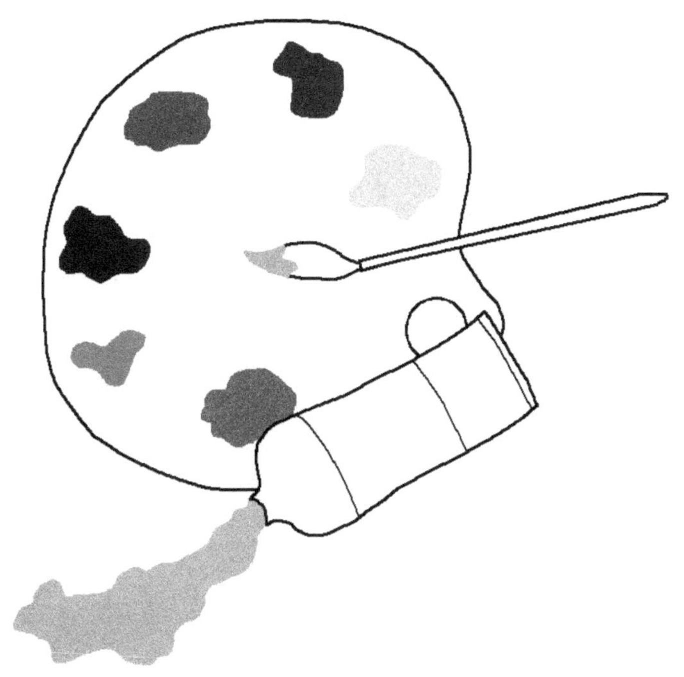

Screaming Silence

Silence like a cage
punctured by rage
Hard to unlock
Harder to escape

Silence like knives
brought on by vibes
of negative emotion
A hateful commotion

Silence like drowning
Taunted by frowning
Hard to swim up
Harder to smile

Silence that's binding
Endlessly trying
to lure you in
You're letting it win

Silence like a coffin
Shut tightly too often
Hard to reopen
Harder to climb out

Silence that's screaming
Builds walls when I'm dreaming
and replaces the spark
with unbreachable dark

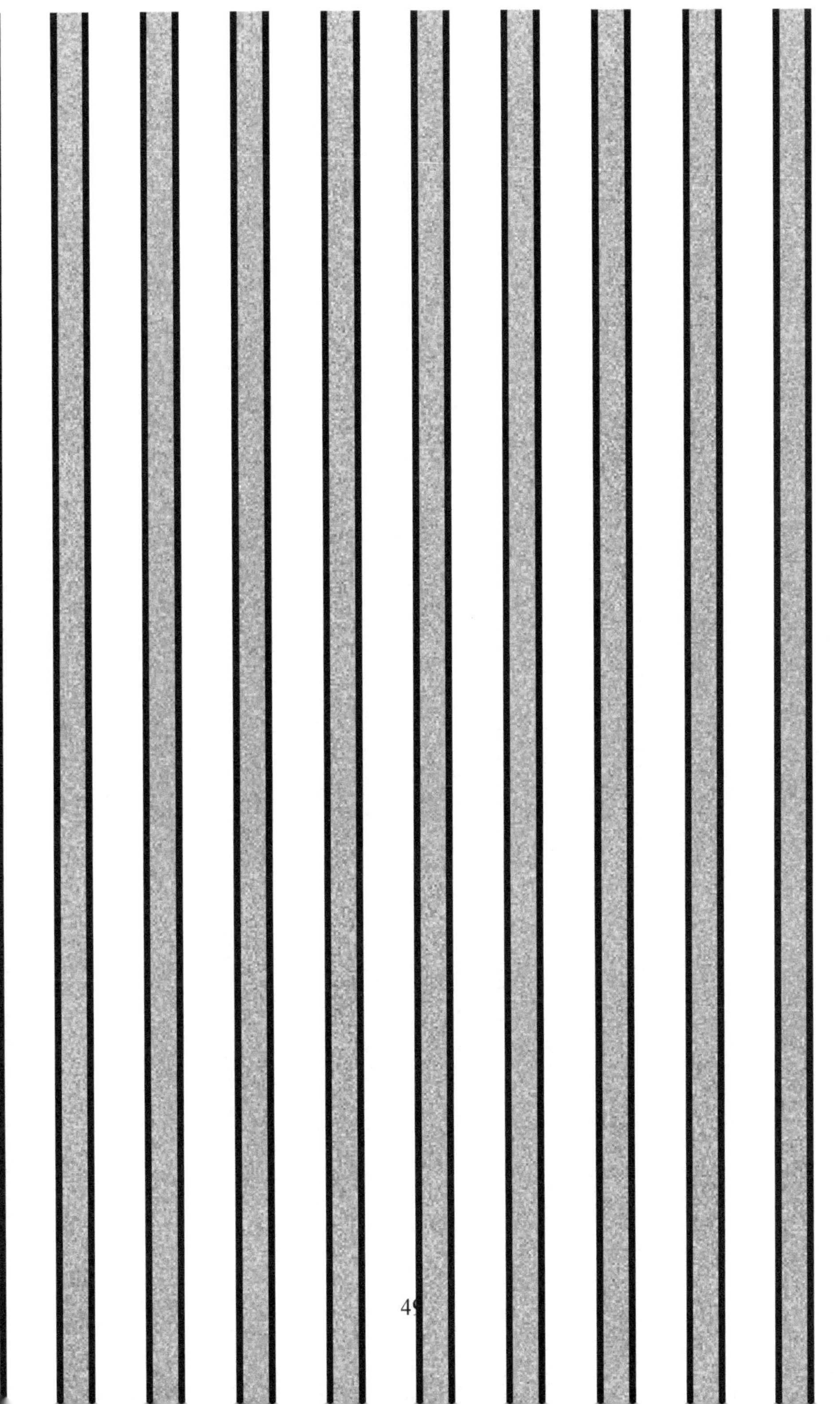

Downfall

I hope you fall
right to the ground
from atop your poison throne
Built from falsehoods
Bound with deceit
Both seeping through your bones

I hope you choke
on lies you speak
as easily as you breathe
Moulded from spite
Tied with rancour
Desperate to deceive

I hope you rot
with all you own
and meet your well-deserved end
Crafted from hate
Woven with rage
No chances to defend

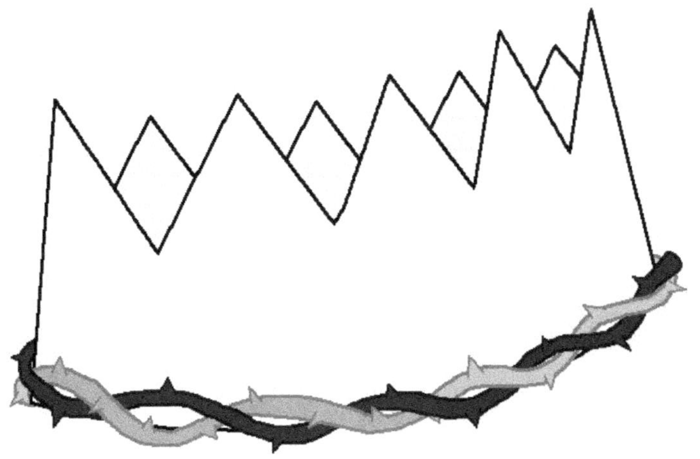

Between North and South: Lies

Part with your morality
and take away my rights
I'll lock the door between us
so I can sleep at night

Empty my remaining trust
Yell as loudly as you can
I'll replay my lost memories
to find how this all began

Tear up my last shreds of hope
and feed them to the birds
I'll find another way to breathe
while choking on your words

Erase my fading dignity
Scream vulgar lines of hate
I'll run away from dreams of you
as my comfort dissipates

Ruin my faith in family
and threaten me lies
I'll keep fighting the ghost of you
until one of us dies

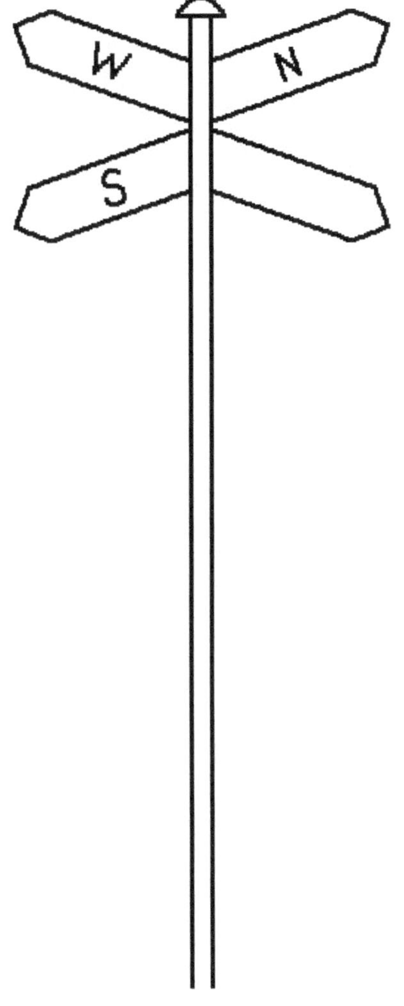

W
N
S

Twisted Shades of Pink

You made me feel like I was strong
when I was stuck feeling lost
and in the time that you've been gone
I break again each day

You helped patch up my damaged mind
with your shards of broken glass
and then left me to stay behind
in the past to fade away

You stole the heart that I had locked
with chains deep in the dark
and swiped the colours I forgot
to turn them into grey

You broke the trust I built for you
with contradicting words
and everything that we'd fought through
would see no time past May

You lied to feel you could belong
in a group that has no bounds
and tell us when we'd spoken wrong
but hurting us was okay

You worried I would disappear
but then you did just that
and reinforced my sturdy fear
that you would never stay

You told me that you'd always care
because you loved me more
and ran while I waited there
but you only cared to play

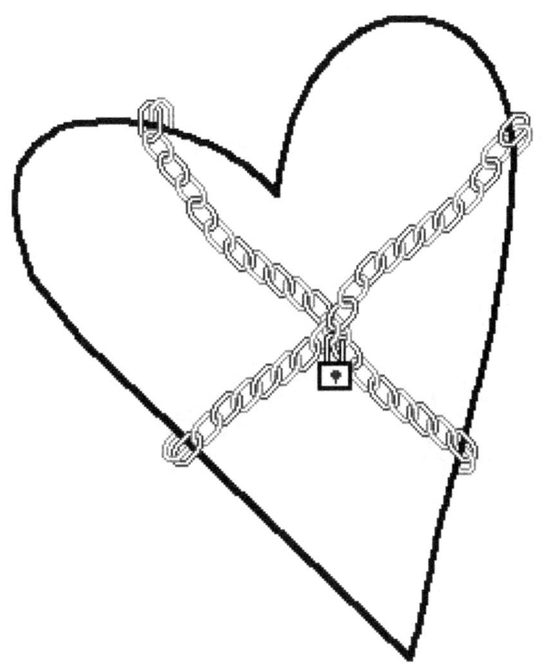

Steps

Tiptoe carefully down the steps
No hazard to self
or risk to be felt
Line the path you take with pillows
You'll never break bones
or feel safest at home

Walk with casual caution down the steps
No over-thinking
or guarded beginning
Leave everything just as it has been
You'll never stay tired
or feel too uninspired

Clamber haphazardly down the steps
No regard for danger
or anything stranger
Abandon the need for a safety net
You'll never refrain
or feel sheltered again
Protected from pain
in a hesitant lane
where you would remain
perfectly comfortable,
and ordinarily sane

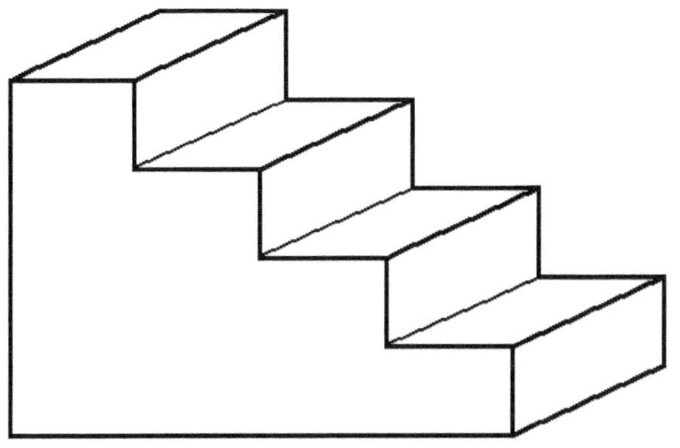

A Good Man

I sometimes find myself wishing you would die
and wondering if I'm as bad as you for that
But all of the hatred you held onto inside
rushed out of you and into my back
So maybe I'm not wrong for hoping you would rot
as flawlessly as the words you spew
Because regardless, if you stay living or not
the fears of your hatred burn true

My father once told me, perhaps in more words,
he'd never wish for death on another
even for someone who brought onslaughts of hurt,
for one who'd made many more suffer
But if the life of a monster was all that it took
to cure the affected of trouble,
it wouldn't be so simple as turning to look
to see millions fall under their rubble

My grandmother hastily defended a man
who took hostage and withheld my rights
Perhaps his actions weren't anyone's plan,
but threats and lies echoed through the nights
Somewhere after darkness, a slur was screamed out,
a door slammed, a step back, a hand almost raised
An accusation flew instead: harsh, blunt, and loud
But all would still defend him, unfazed

My uncle had sworn that his dad wasn't "bad"
but do good people do what he did?
Would a good man take away rights as he had?
Would a good man put my life at risk?
If a good man could lie and threaten and swear,
if a good man would make others fear,
would it make me a bad man to foster and care?
Would a good or bad man be sincere?

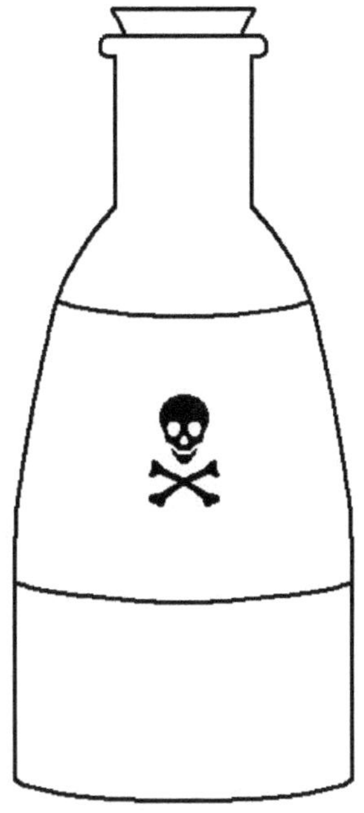

A Brain Full of Static

Encumbered with anxiety that claws at my mind,
ripping thoughts into shreds that get harder to find
and I can't place the moment I started to slip
into this feeling that's so much like a pit

Smothered by sadness that clings to my bones,
covering hopes with a blanket of groans
and I can't take it off when it's pinned down so tight
bringing more darkness when I needed the light

Haunted by memories that trample my lungs,
crushing them firmly so my breath comes undone
and I struggle to catch it when it leaves so fast
while I try to remember the feeling won't last

Imprisoned by feelings that lock down my brain,
echoes taking my will to replace it with pain
and I try to do what I can out of spite
for all of the people that made me need to fight

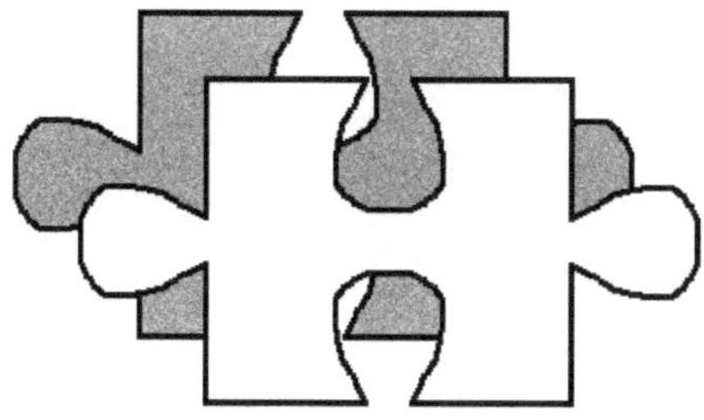

A Friend in Death

Death came to find me, I begged him to stay
"I'm tired of being in pain every day"
But Death shook his head as he started to leave
"The pain doesn't last, I hope you'll believe"
So Death walked away and left me alone
and I told all my troubles to find a new home

Death came to find me, I begged him to go
"I've finally found what I needed to grow"
But Death turned to me and he gave me a smile
"I'm just checking in, your time's not for a while"
So Death gave a wave, wished me well as he went
and I understood what the words spoken had meant

Death will return to find me one day
far in the future to take me away
But Death isn't evil, that's far from the truth,
just doing his job, the same way we all do
So Death won't come early, he helped me survive
and when the time comes, we'll know I was ALIVE

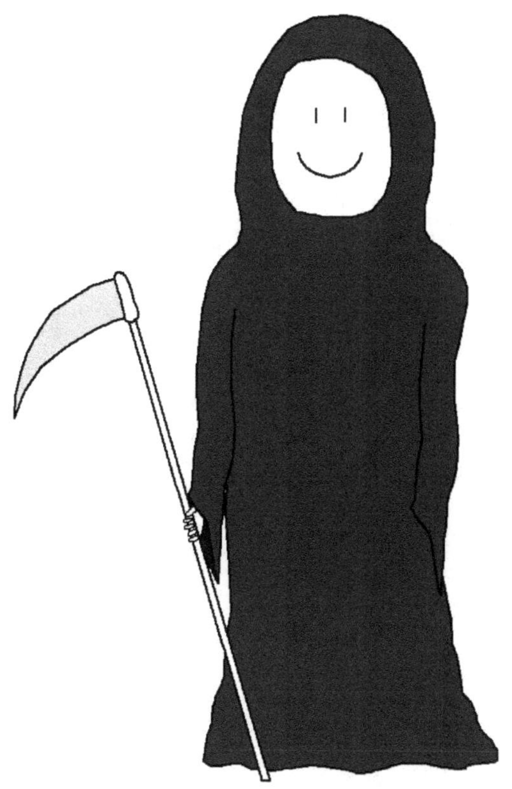

The Liar Plant

You can water the liar plant, but you can't make it grow
If it chooses, it can weave its way right into your soul
You can try to guide the thirsty into the waterfall,
but if the liar got them first then they're sure to make you
crawl
You can take the hungry, lead them right to the buffet
Just hold hope the liar hasn't shown them another way
See, the liar, he is cunning, he's determined to survive
He will do whatever's necessary just to stay alive
But the liar stays a liar, as a liar's always been
and every way he has deceived you will remain unseen
See, the liar told a story, one to make himself look good
but the truth is sure to come out, as a liar's always would
Perhaps you'll understand then how a liar plays his game
but if you still believe it, you're a liar all the same

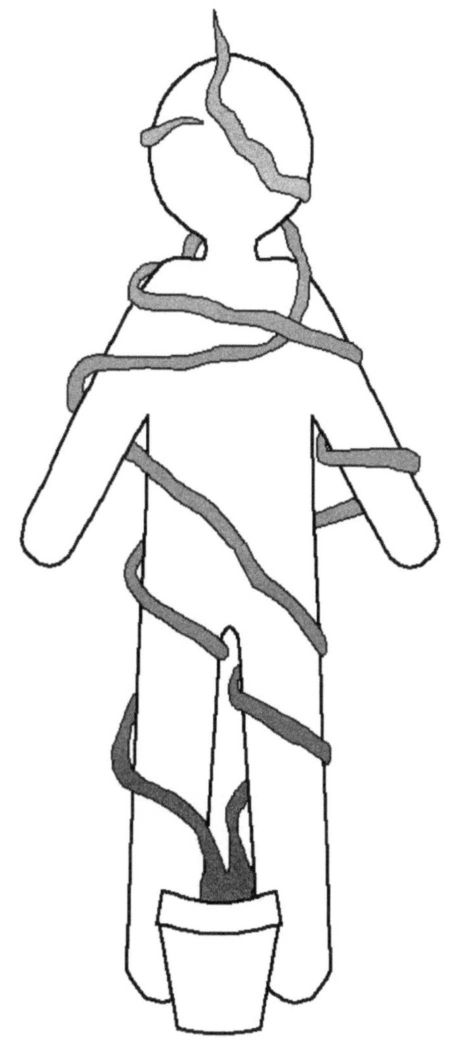

Grow

I feel like my brain is missing
Feels like I've been away too long
Never taking, always giving
until things start going wrong

And I try so fucking hard
to fix all of my mistakes
Sometimes I need to know I can't
but everyone around just takes

They take away my safety,
like he took away my rights
She took away all I'd need
to sleep right through the nights

Maybe it never mattered
to anyone but me
But my dreams have all been shattered,
not knowing when I'll be free

I fought to keep myself alive
the way they fight to hide the truth
All while falling, losing time
to claims I don't have proof

I would tape my mouth closed
but I would soon suffocate
The memories would choke
with the words fuelled with hate

My mind feels like static
when it used to be strong
While the reflex to panic
screams everything is wrong

So when does it get better?
When do they begin to see?
What I lost, I lost together
What I've gained, I got from me

Rage builds like fire in my heart
Fury burns inside my chest
for everything they tore apart,
discarded with the rest

Now everything remaining
feels distant and a blur
Like reading road signs while it's raining
I feel like I'm never sure

Because everything I lost
is something that I can't get back
and if my heart starts to defrost
will I still stay on the track?

Like a train that's losing grip
Like a child that's being born
Like the energy that will tip
when a new day starts its dawn

And if I lost my way
would you even know?
Or would it be okay
that they stole my chance to grow?

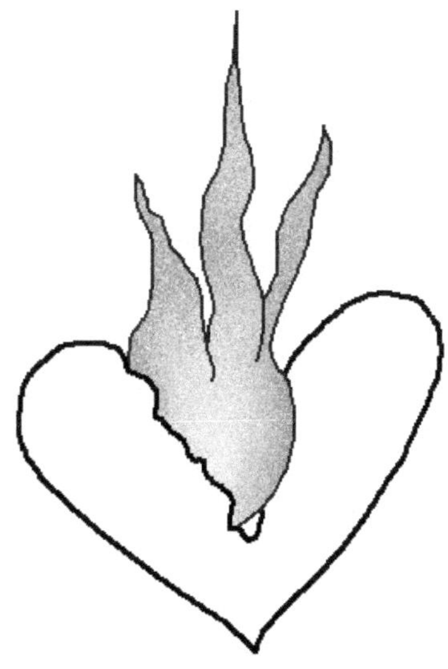